EXIT STRATEGY

Patrick Wright is an award-winning poet from Manchester, UK. His poems have appeared in *Poetry Ireland Review*, *The North*, *Gutter*, *Poetry Salzburg*, *Agenda*, and *The London Magazine*. His debut pamphlet, *Nullaby*, was published in 2017 by Eyewear. His debut full-length collection, *Full Sight of Her*, was published in 2020 by Eyewear and nominated for the John Pollard Prize. He has been shortlisted for the Bridport Prize and twice included in *The Best New British and Irish Poets* anthology. He teaches English and Creative Writing at the Open University.

Also by Patrick Wright

Full Sight of Her   (Eyewear, 2020)

Nullaby   (Eyewear, 2017)

Fallen Pictures   (Oneiros Books, 2013)

For Kim & Rowan

ISBN: 978-1-916938-71-7

Cover designed by Aaron Kent

Edited and Typeset by Aaron Kent

Broken Sleep Books Ltd
PO BOX 102
Llandysul
SA44 9BG

CONTENTS

Exit Strategy

Patrick Wright

Broken Sleep Books

You will burn, and you will burn out; you will be healed and come back again.

— Fyodor Dostoevsky

LIMINAL WORLDS
After Maria Popova

When so much of you is a smog-filled sky
the causeway extends towards skyscrapers

half-demolished
when birds fly off precognitively from window ledges

I re-script my dreams in which you're alive

In the split second between fireball & thunder
I imagine a white rhino is born

In the moment between morphine & biopsy
at least one elevator is caught

one silhouette snatched head-first out of the furnace

In the instant between syringe & stitch
a white dress is gifted

between a single cell & metastasis
those stars   stapling your waist   string a line of kisses

BEGINNING OR END
After Idris Khan

I dreamt of a butterfly the size of a dinner plate.
It seemed to breathe the truth of rebirth across my face
& I believe in a reassembly.

I want to break God's leg, stamp on it endlessly.
I want everything in flames, to end it all
in a dance of worlds, a Nemesis collision.

Did you know colours aren't there? Everything is black
before photons fall on a postage stamp. I want
my eye to behold the antipodes.

I want to prise open the doors ...
& ask: *is this a hologram?* Are its pixels too small?
At times I touch the rope & the alarm goes off.

I torment myself with *I couldn't save you—*
& yet I saved you.
Death is the one thing we can truly own.

METANOIA

This is not your destruction—
            For a star to ignite its centre & shower the vacuum
with light, remember a cloud must first collapse & go on
                                   collapsing
like a breakdown.
            No, not madness—torn apart by change
tin soldiers melt & form a heart, now laying in a hearth
                  like a cinder from the Wormwood Star.
I can't stop thinking of Oppenheimer & a blast radius
                mannequins scorched in a paper town.
I can't seem to transform myself—
              I learned the first law of thermodynamics
believed in retrograde, you'd return like a meteorite
      that tumbles through sleep, dissolves on impact.
             Don't ask me to find meaning in Cassiopeia.
I can't share your eyes—the stars: pinholes through a tarp.
              Why do parts of a galaxy spin at the same speed?
             God—please tell me
glial cells are the brain's dark matter—the sun's tilt
              through a star field
is more than the elliptic
          & from Mauna Kea there's such a thing as omens at least.
I think of robots deserting us
        at a distance—& in this paint, the stellar debris.

VIR HEROICUS SUBLIMIS
After Barnett Newman

Forget meaning for the Greeks & Christ the man or Christ who is God

or cathedrals conceived as such; witness one field of consciousness

where zips are light beams of mortals. Perhaps heaven is like this & colour

goes on till colour has nothing to fall upon. Ask yourself about 'red' & qualia.

Some would see 'blue' here. When we perceive a magic trick takes place:

the image gets flipped & thrown & appears on the back of the brain.

No conjurer in the occipital lobe or ghost in the machine, no homunculus.

So much beyond the visible surrounds the frame & yet so little

like seeing only a single strip when gazing across the Mississippi River.

SHROUD

After Shirazeh Houshiary

In the last few hours, we are young again:
our eyes go wide like a baby's & we unlearn
verbs & nouns. Some see little people
& distant bells are heard through side walls.

You clawed at sheets, tried to eat inedible
things, while grief *is* a human experience.

In the dark, I panthered to each breath,
as though each breath were your last.

Now in the dark with the avant-garde
it's just the same: the embers of stars
in otherwise black squares, while on this
side I have nothing beyond my instinct.

BLACK SQUARE REDUX
After Kazimir Malevich

Let's forget God   & build machines to resurrect the dead
let's resist the flesh   & praise the third law of thermodynamics
repeat what Nietzsche said   though let's proceed with tenderness
All the cavalcade of -isms   they did nothing but circle the abyss
I want icons to stay in bits   tea leaves to reveal the Antichrist
Let's re-create the Kingdom of Heaven here   & not rely on faith
be cosmonauts   & reanimate the space-strewn molecules of our
ancestors   colonise planets when the Earth is full of revenants
All my love   only now do I know   was a struggle against entropy
I was a futurist when I prayed by your bed   dreaming of machines
to save your brain's neurones & synapses   even though those zeros
exceed the stars in the universe   machines to upload your genes
be able to trace & reattach   each piece of ash scattered on a beach
What though if the dead want to stay dead   like in *Star Trek*
Is a body that beams or teleports the same body   or a clone
Would we get bored of ourselves   after aeons of living with our
faults   & would we have to be cyborgs   once our limbs wore out
If no babies were born   would humans be human anymore

COLD ROOM
After Mary Corse

Beyond the argon and plexiglas I know of another cold room.
As I move through the doorway,

through her use of light tubes and a high-frequency generator,
I am my own cold room.

This is the installation view—despite the refrigeration panels
I am seeing a different cold room.

Here with the monofilament and a compressor, I am at a loss
in this cold room.

White noise like a broken television. I am the broken television
unable to receive a signal.

I find tiny glass microspheres, the kind used to paint white lines
on asphalt roads in the cold room,

which animate the surface of blank windows, such as *Untitled*.
I too am untitled in this cold room.

I too keep cold—and under fluorescents there is nothing new.

DARK CLOUDS STORM BLUE

Another cloud is the archive of photos. I upload them with voice notes
& they're fragile. They do not live in heaven; they dwell in the desert & can burn
anytime. If they were in a hard drive, I'd send them into orbit around Saturn—
out of reach of when the sun expands. They say grief is like a cloud
& though it stays the same size we somehow grow around it. I strain hard
to find a face—then, glowering eyes & mouths. They move like boxcars.

Dark clouds on my ceiling hover so close & the storm is blue, this kind
of blue always sounds like a cello or jazz in the early hours. In my sleep
I saw her corpse turn into snow, & I worry over where the self goes.
When the merging comes. On sailing ships these clouds cast shadows
& drag like bedclothes over my back. Meanwhile, the sun is a great absence:
an eye gazing through the cloudiness of its cataract.

I am a fool to look for patterns where no patterns reside. I am a sucker
for confirmation bias. I can no longer laugh at these legless sheep.
Behind the clouds is the mirror of the Pacific in the evening, miles from
the nearest atoll. I am shrouded by the sky. I foresee lightning; it comes
like scissors down silk & rips as hands rip a dress. I see lipstick on the mirror—
a kiss—her deliberate phantom. Someone should be answerable for this.

NEGATIVE SPACE
After Rachel Whiteread

I wake in a panic   imagining all the new people
wearing your clothes   As I cleared out your snug
every star of glitter   seemed salvageable

Things that caused pain   two years ago
I now have on my windowsill

I glimpse photos   as though we've spoken
       just before

My malady consists   in how I cannot keep
two worlds in opposition

       The membrane between sleep
and waking   permeable

Your mother told you to leave   after a while

Such visits give succour   What's hard is living
once touched with fire

AN EXPLODED VIEW
Alongside Cornelia Parker

                                          hinged

brackets   spin   in a vortex

still   as a supernova   remnant

pine-lap panels   stripped   by wasps

hung   on fishing wires   just because

if I learn   to love   the bomb

perhaps   it will look   like this

fixed   in a millisecond   like smiles

in jpegs   on   external drives

          at my

          centre is

          a single

          lightbulb

now   a sky-dance   of swallows

or galaxies   just   fly apart

your toys   tools   left behind clothes

your LPs   all screaming   *let me go*

EXIST STRATEGY
After the last photograph she took from her hospital bed

I stab a knife in a kitchen's surface—an existential protest. Or an artist's statement?

I tried to fight & the assailant was invisible.

Now even baby carriages stink of nihilism.

I confide *I want the whole world to burn.*

I'm sick of being a plaything of the gods. They pull my strings just because.

They're capricious & wrong to leave us with such quandaries.

I want to fight with Zeus.

I reckon if I pump my muscles up, I'll go the distance.

I'd like to haymaker the door to be heard in Hades.

I beat my pillow with my fist. Here is the heart space.

Awaiting blood tests was like Russian roulette. I won't be scared again.

Ours was a war I couldn't win.

Now I know it destroys all I invest—like a toddler attacked by a dog, handcuffed to a fence.

I could do nothing save for making ice pops. I made the best ice pops.

I wanted to jump on a hand grenade, & no hand grenade.

No more chemical cures, swimming in ice, helplines ...

Friends accuse me of self-sabotage.

I resent the re-wiring taking place—how it's change or die.

I am the wound & the blade.

TRUE BELIEF BELONGS TO THE REALM OF REAL KNOWLEDGE
After Idris Khan

I believe our lives go on inside a tesseract.

In dreams we make love & amnesia stops me wanting to stay.

I believe if I wait long enough, till the end, you'll return as a saviour.

I believe in Orphic descents, & dreams are encrypted, & dreams
are between here & the place we belong.

I agree with Bohm: that the Andromeda spiral could be curled inside
one of our teardrops.

In the realm between quarks, everything occurs.

I believe this room doesn't exist till we look at it.

I agree with Augustine: that time makes sense till we think it through.

If time's a river, how do we know the water moves?

If we're not flesh & something else, why choose Earth?

Why is the Moon in just the right place?

I believe in leaving our shadows to step outside the cave.

I believe that death means falling out of time, & living the same life
over & over again.

∞

COLD DARK MATTER
After Cornelia Parker

Thanks to you I am learning to see again
through a sparseness of particles—

like how I learned to listen to an eyelid
twitch once *yes* and twice *no* through a coma.

Darkness I've come to realise is a privilege—
known at 4am & sleepless

the sun rising like a scalpel
& turning the room purple.

Somehow, we go on & somehow it never ends
& we go on like a double pendulum.

Perhaps love is like this fixed explosion.
Perhaps you're nearer now than the word *belief.*

SEVERANCE
After Aisha Khalid

I hear it's rather like a firewall	that was Swedenborg
& here is	the womb
where Mozart	can't get
through	I am
told the	butterfly
never returns	to the
chrysalis	the veil
to me	says some
things must	remain sacred
or some	things
cannot be	shouldn't be
represented	I will
assume	not to know
is in my	best interests
I was	punching doors
to have	my voice
heard by	Hades
It seems	so very
wrong	that we're
not allowed	to talk
instead the blue light of a device	mediates us

TENEBRAE

The first question I'll ask the angels is why do the dead
feel the need to desert us.

I sighed your candle out and the grills were silent.

I gazed at the flame and hoped for a conduit.

I received the gift of tears. I received, while *they* prayed.

For now, the priest is the next best thing—so I ask why
our speech is prohibited.

To slap a priest would be reprehensible. Why can't they
find a dog's soul through its eyes?

And when the last candle goes out, I've journeyed far
and still, we're unrequited.

I wonder if God is saying I must go through him
to get to you.

They say it's just a transition: from one body to another.

I've no patience for the psalms—each candle snuffed out.

If science is a candle in the dark, this must be what it means
to see while blind.

I've had all over the body shivers—though like a favourite
song is playing with rhythms curled in my cochlea.

This gradual extinguishing is like our body's functions.

Death is a process and never like Hollywood.

Then the strepitus comes like a rumble of thunder.

Then the lights go up and the candelabra casts the shadow
of a spider on the wall.

A DISTANT FAWN

Off in the glades, a fawn crouches, hears its own
heartbeat, a wolf upwind. & still a whole field
killed by lightning. Orphans search for mother's
scent, before their heads sprout into branches.

Was it God in disguise?—the fawn at Darsham
Marshes. Ghost-like, going off. It seemed to say
I'm here, don't follow. By the trees we glimpsed
a whorl of fur, receding further as we stepped.

My lips on your forehead. I was a fawn in your
limbus. I was going off, going off in the distance.

JARDIN LA NUIT
After Paul Klee

Woodlice, unswept, under the slipshod leaves.
Solar lights switching on across the yard
like Orion's belt, & a jack-o-lantern.

I paint a doll white, bury her for Persephone,
find a pergola & a bridge leading nowhere,
a crescent hanging with cooler hues.

Where do bluebottles sleep after they crash
into glass?—the same place the dead go
if they've not accepted Christ?

When the sky is purple, it's time to cry.
The shrubs are better off without me,
the ivy doing its thing, unsheared.

I reach for digitalis & count fallen sparrows
in this garden where statues come to life,
& the trees are singed with catastrophe.

SHADOW OF A GIRL PLAYING WITH A HULA HOOP
After Giorgio de Chirico

It used to scare me, what this girl is doing,
or those around her, off in the blind field.
Seemingly a girl playing with a hula hoop,
or just a shadow, no source, just a shadow
next to a wagon, its backdrop here a dusty
plaza. Somewhere, I feel, from an upstairs
room, an eye looks at me. Somewhere, off
screen, a murder is taking place, this shade
a clue. Even so, things are too belated now,
this girl clearly a phantom and not a muse,
like she's in a toy shop or inside its puzzle,
no girl playing so nonchalant with a hoop.
The sun, at these times, is no longer a sun,
more likely a lamp. My fingers are syllables.
And this pine table where the postcard sits
is full of knots, staring like gods from above.

DEATH OF ORPHEUS
After Henri-Léopold Lévy

Forensics are on their way with their tent:
they'll dust my stump for fingerprints.

My limbed torso clings to its Android case.
My severed head buoyant. Blue grey paint.

The hoodies scarper—a gang-filmed frenzy
for a mobile app: The Maenads.

This upper world harsh in its heaviness.
She's gone, I know, like a voice down a well.

Thrace, a landscape, holds on to mysteries
where clouds unfurl like bandages.

The water laps.
Notes blow and whistle through the branches.

It's too late to ask: How far should I take this?

ROBERT RAUSCHENBERG'S *UNTITLED*

& already I see alpines
prise their way through the brutalist grey
of Chernobyl floors. Through the sarcophagus
they reach for sunlight. Maybe we only learn
what the burn of graphite means once blind.
I know you better after knowing disaster.

I've studied the colour theories
of Goethe and Albers where the wheel
& the wheel of life are a way to feel closer.
I am the stalk through the fallout, one that insists
on pushing its way & one that's been patient.
On the surface we share the mark of detonation.

They say a town like this is void
though one pulse of a deer's heart
makes it a plenum. A full spectrum will reveal
itself only when you've pledged to cease
hurting. Through this I see what you saw
when the sun set & made shades on a radiator.
We are both on the side of art.

UNTYING THE SCARF

You're with me now
like a swan's shadow.
With me, like a blindfold pulled closer.

For you, it was a joke & simulacrum:
how I grabbed for a switch & felt the implosion—
a submarine at crush depth.

While, off screen, in the blind field
you watched like an aristocrat
having passed through forever.

Unravelling the organza,
I was a failure & your distant admirer.
In our universe of two, it was a miracle.

LEGACY
After Vincent Van Gogh

Just like how
I wake
to a rebus
or sense
something
needs to
be said
even though
I said
just about
everything
my dreams
find you
& there
you ghost
me—calls
unanswered
like I'm
your stalker.

A cassette
was left
behind of
Kurt Vonnegut
in the
afterlife.
A room
of ciphers.
Easter eggs—
like how
the wall's
sunflower
seems to
throw his
voice from
Arles or
his hand
is a ruse
& a phantom.

NIGHT SEA JOURNEY

It seems you've left me floating in the Sea of Cortez.
Left with after-effects, torso upturned to the stars.
My bed surrounded by a carpet, the ocean's depths,

I wonder from where the light of dreams emanates.
How shadows are cast in the cortex. Other realities
are as close as your jugular vein. So says the Koran.

On the verge of jumping after you, what stops me?
I've made an altar, placed trigger objects—
amulets to amplify the residue, the mind an aerial.
I've burnt incense, switched devices to record ...

By the morning sun, the lounge is transfigured. I listen
for raps, hear floorboards expand, a distant siren
or the sound a mother makes after the death of a child.

BLACK ON MAROON
After Mark Rothko

1
Some leaves look like this,
matt on tarmac.

They glint where rain pools.
All is camouflage.

What else but a window,
sill consumed by shadows.

The black, liquorice-like.
The light is sherbet.

A car is maroon;
organ walls, tissue ...

What's left after the sky
left its prophecy.

The damask of the room
on the wicker divide.

Black on black, a single fishnet
which isn't mine.

Black on black are the wigs,
now no one's at all.

2

Such colours, the shade
of funeral balloons—

mauves, maroons.
And light: the kind that enters

through a snail's broken shell.
In this place the pronouns

are incinerated, walls close
in with incremental force.

Like a party where all
the guests have left, where

through the blinds
sleeplessness is reaching

towards distant cars.
How your scarf droops

to an innocent smile—
how the planets

promise to rise,
though fall again.

WINTER LANDSCAPE WITH SKATERS AND BIRD TRAP
After Pieter Bruegel the Elder

I find no pleasure in the ice.
Everything about me lies still—save for murmurations.

Peasants weave between trees: each crystalline
like coral on a seabed.

I give you a winter landscape in place of a mirror.
The bird trap is my heart.

Soon it will be still, a skull in a crypt, lit by candles.
My hills are a wishbone. They undulate under great tension.

The skaters are insouciant, crows peck their shadows.
My face startles—a chance alignment of stars.

Skaters are on slippery ground
and if they should slip, they have nothing to cling onto.

ABSTRACTION

the greatest truths I've found are
that god is a ladybird in disguise

                                     Hades will remain mute to my protests
after the apocalypse I must nail
meaning down through inscape

                                the choice to go on living arrives
when I feel vertigo over a cliff

                             the sound of immanence can be heard
as the rain blitzkriegs my glass

                              one meaning of martyr is to bear witness
when I save a snail on the pavement
I save humanity

                            at least Christ only had one crucifixion
I need a ghost in the machine

                                   science is just a line of paradigms
I need my black swans and white crows

                               my words must serve as a requiem
love is beyond Aristotle's categories

                            all these are variations on a theme

∞

LARGE BLUE (EXTINCT)

Against a black background the large blue stills its wings. It wasn't pinned here. The blue's dragged out of a dream like Novalis' blue flower. It speaks, says *this is my new face—I have transitioned.* Compound eye, do you see me now, my fate, my heart pounding with hurt & holding on, & longing so intently, nailed to your gaze

from my locket photograph?

Antenna, can you hear my

thoughts, can you receive everything I ever said, in body, you never did quite hear? Am I deaf to signals? After all, am I invisible or just extinct—a man weeping seemingly for no reason, lost in a museum, desperate for the blue to be your avatar, a postcard of how nothing departs?

BLACK SQUARE
After Kazimir Malevich

In this light   the surface is a black mirror   I don't want to see
myself seeing back   not seeing black   Behind cut glass a black
cat in a coal bunker   fur curled in a corner   Learn to see flat
see flatly   the way Freud listened   Does matt paint glisten
a sea-creature?   or is this Vantablack   sense deprivation
an anechoic chamber?   The only sound is the nervous system
heart hurtling inside my cranium   Here I see the starlessness
between galaxies   the black   of nothing quite happening
of consciousness closing   fastening   Could this be a *Madonna
and Child*   figures excised   (Suprematist and still   a mother
and child)?   This black   has a dead Christ uncanniness
(Holbein's panel for Prince Myshkin)   This is also Gallipoli
field artillery (out into history)   Closer   this is only a semblance
of black   a rainbow   the web of a shattered phone
A buffalo torso legs   a head hurrying towards some wilderness

THE GREY PEOPLE
Alongside Diane Arbus

Such greyscale smiles
worn by aristocrats
who've passed by privilege

Blank as a clock face
under midnight fluorescents
Her cripples, her stars

This giant stoops low
Light bulb scorching curls
parents small as dolls

Nudists in armchairs
lounge beside blinds
Flash: atomic sunlight

Hermaphrodite and
lapdog in a carnival
house, lips behind glass

Adore the drag artist
dancing with suited guy
Face lost in her breast

All wheel-chaired ones
in bag-head costumes
gathered for Samhain

Thumb over her lens
Sword-swallowing albino
Christ tattooed, arms wide

Twins side by side
eyes unblinking
Hands: resting damselflies

Girl with a cigar
in Washington Square Park
Ash about to fall

A dwarf, butt naked
save for trilby and tache
escaping her circus

Flaws blown up large
through her aperture
this closed-door sideshow

for me: the sole voyeur

NOCTURNE
After James McNeill Whistler

Over the Thames are ghost trails of rockets
reflecting like stars on the water's edge—
cinders showering down, a Rorschach test.

They say this is a cause to celebrate:
the paint vague, stirring the mind's slideshow—
dabs of green, yellow. They double, cascade,

coalesce into a Manhattan by night.
Or are they strip-lights seen through fabric?
Much begins with deliberate accidents.

Spectators gaze, blinkered by their habits.
Pale to themselves, not quite transparent.
In the courtroom, it was hung upside down.

SUNRISE WITH SEA MONSTERS
After J.M.W. Turner

Some see sails. A dog's head, a float,
icebergs, a fishing net, a steam-driven paddleboat?
Forms coalesce, a single behemoth.

Hiding is their habit, latent under waves.
They emerge as swirls, curios.
No one is sure what they are.

Nose tips, fins. Whatever exists, more than fish.
It borders on a colour field, yellows and golds.
In the yellows: madness and wallpaper.

How the blind might see the world
if the gift of sight were suddenly returned.
A retinal flash, God (almost).

The mind finds its mirror. It's a thermal process.
As if the self were a nimbus—drifting steam, vortices.

LESSONS ON HOW TO VIEW A MONDRIAN

First glance simple, though it's a masquerade.
Off-white, black stripes, pale lemon. The canvas
is the whole universe, with nothing beyond it.
Stop and a world unfurls from a bud: scarabs,
teeth, X-rays, halos. Luscious surfaces, rubbed
to a weave. At the borders of stripes, they aren't
just lines where black meets white or blue or
yellow. At the cordon you'll see how he's changed

his mind. If you bend down, look up against the
light, it shows the warp and weft at forty-five
degrees to stripes. A closer look shows a stairway
of paint. In some parts, there's been no paper to
guide him. He's kept his hand from wavering,
joyed in the tremble and feints. When you put
up an easel in a museum, everyone talks to you.
          If you sit and write a poem, nobody does.

POSTCARD: *UNTITLED*
Before Mark Rothko

As the floor gives way, I'm a bird always burning up
in the desert. Every few years, I tear off my layers.
I eat the ashes of predecessors.
I'm the torment of cells, neural connections.

I've learned the process: like a river the flow
in my veins is never the same twice. If you stare
into me, you'll pay the price.
I'll wear the halo; you keep your distance.

I'll push through the prison bars of your eyelashes.
Whiteness around me—the bleached surface of a
cistern. Like me it's sterile. I'm the augury of a cut
finger—how it pools. My pain exquisite as a stingray.

I offer no trigger warning, no disclaimer.
I'm coming at you with a switchblade.

PORTRAIT OF KATHERINE MANSFIELD
Alongside Anne Rice

I never dreamt of coughing blood the colour of this dress.
Nor spending the English winters abroad. I only dreamt
of ending stories abruptly, using words the way a cello rises
and falls. As a girl my dreams were an atlas. To escape windy
Wellington, leave on a liner, find my fictive home. I wrote
of jazzy palettes, low-neck bohemian garb. How life could
be all syntax, experiment. From Wilde's prose and a Māori
breast, I adored the fetish, torn between gestalt and imago.
My red dress fills most of the canvas. As an émigré, I'd share
a cigarette, strut in a kimono. At parties, I'd laud suffragettes
or write vignettes in bold strokes like the Fauves. Aroused,
I'd return from the colonies, my personas piling like a house
of cards. I'd be polyamorous, endless rhythm. I'd embody
the fleeting and contingent. In the end, I'd ride a falling star.

MEMENTO MORI
After doing the Holbein thing

Lacan wrote of a ghost that hides between pages &
love as turning inside-out the finger of a glove. A
skull reveals itself as I glance into the room & make
for the exit. It's never face-on: i.e., anamorphic.
Like a spider on a wall shocks, a crack in the fabric
of existence, a mandible intrudes & gnaws a vacuum.
As if gravity has warped, elongated light around the bone.
Its bald white flight scares me to the edge of blackout.
Every paradise after all has a serpent coiled. So, I fall
into one of its sockets, a black hole orbiting another.
A hyper-mindfulness won't help matters: to impress
the fact, the glass is already broken. & so, I'll fall back
into repression, forget how the nasal gap offers itself
like an entrance. How its laughter will one day be my own.

THE MISOPHONIC BRAIN

would prefer the colour blue,
a world curled inside a swirl
like Kandinsky's canvas, blue
gyres, lines forming a syntax, a blue
haven inside a spectrum, a blue
triangle or river-walk to infinity,
or tangles like a blue disco wig,
electric blue flicker to the tunes.
The path he pursues towards blue
is heading to the absolute, the blue
star shining brighter white like Rigel,
the clue of the divine. I am blue
under birdsong, when baby shrieks
pierce me in cafés. In the blue
I hear no chord sequence, rhythms
or E minors. I listen, though blue,
towards the still crystal blue
of a pool, towards the blue
of its sky-mirror, where blue
lifts me now beyond measure.

ARCHIVE
After Anselm Kiefer

Before his landscapes scorched by war and history, paintings of straw
and glue, *your golden hair, Margarethe*, before 'Death Fugue', I was back at
school, deep winter. In the yard blew a few stray crisp packets; seagulls
pecked at crumbs. The annex and fence had the look of an abandoned
camp, in Polish hinterlands. Through a cloakroom window I peered,
looking for a ghost of myself, then at a ghost of myself, as the sun
poked out from a cloud and the contours of bulimia gazed back, in
sepia tones. I saw the bullies too, with razored eyebrows, piercings,
fists in my gut, spit on my shoulder, the stench of Lynx, using *queer*
as an insult. With my SLR, I clicked more in hope than expectation.
I fumbled with fixative, the stop bath, the gelatin swell. My negatives
solarised. I kept re-visiting as a witness. Those days, I bit the inside
of my lip, stubbed cigarettes out on my arm. When the dysmorphic
class photos were framed, still as that winter, *your golden hair*, said the
Kiefer print, *your golden hair, Margarethe.*

THE DREAM
After Henri Rousseau

Like a somnambulist I wander through plates. In a daze
the eye of the elephant peers between leaves.

Like in the jungles of his last decade
I am captive in place of something exotic or sensual.

Beside the standard nude and highbrow porn
I am the elephant in the gloom. In a daze

through hot house fronds and lotus flowers
I am desperate to evade the lion.

I am centre-stage and charmed by a musician in shade.
Always a snake curled in paradise. In a daze

I imagine a soirée with Édouard Manet. I exist in a cage —
or escape far away to oneiric evocations.

I exist in a mundane landscape. I exist
in a room—on the page. In a daze—though waking soon—

I exist where the neighbours are afraid to look.

PROVIDENCE, RHODE ISLAND
Alongside Francesca Woodman

To return in autumn

                    is to hide behind a fireplace

slip under a sheet of wallpaper.

                    I twirled nude through rooms

lived for the lens of a Yashica reflex.

                    Since adolescence

I used a mirror to see between my legs.

                    I preferred a single shot:

to blur a trace of the subject.

                    I wore damask like a shroud.

The aperture:

                    a whirlpool through which I could fall.

I drowned

                    & caught bubbles as they escaped my lips.

In Rome

                    I spent too long studying a stain under an architrave.

I never came back.

                    My arms held out in front of me like a somnambulist.

I'd hang myself

                    from lintels in cruciform pose. I never had a house

to haunt.

                    I was the true Baroque. I'd wander up a staircase

like Nosferatu

                    play hide-and-seek till the boyfriends left me.

I adored puppets:

                    how they swung.

My immurements

                    made me believe in magic.

The house devoured me.

I'm seeing the after-image.

How I clipped on angel wings

till the answer appeared.

Here I am in pages.

Here I am

Penelope

                    reweaving   her tapestries.

ASCENT OF THE BLESSED
After Hieronymus Bosch

Hovering a hundred feet over an ambulance
in the starless dark, they congregate.
Below: a machine frantic to restart my heart.
My silver cord stretches, doesn't quite snap.

I look down on the mad scurry:
whatever I am is *not* my body.
A presence beckons, makes it all seem like a painting.
I forget the paramedics massaging my cardiac muscle.

Are those seraphs? How do they levitate?
I can't tell if they're drugged or lulled.
I can't tell if that's bliss on their faces
or gapes of protest. Do we have a choice?

Perhaps this corridor is a vulva in reverse.
Perhaps the womb is a two-way door.
Beyond thought: no stopping-off point.
I look at the craquelure, and say this is art.

MY SERIES OF LONG GOODBYES

Retinitis sounds like a cool sea-creature.
I photographed a sunset on a radiator.
Imagine a shape seared by an atomic flash
or a Cubist nude behind frosted glass.
I was never a man who destroys canvases.
I was scarified by well-meaning acts.
Since memories of childhood surgeries
always trying to rip off the bandages
I'd scratch the itch at the back of my eye.
My field reduced to the size of a bruise.
Imagine the moon through a cataract.
Imagine nothing but a private abstract.
Last summer's moths all bleached out.
So many things I wish you'd never seen
like how porn distorts the female form.

Where I am now has the full spectrum.
Where I am is devoid of white canes and sunglasses.
Where I am is where a woman can gaze
Where you cannot turn round and look straight back.

PRIVATE VIEWING

I'm a nuisance, a disturbance to curators. Arriving at reception, I've
asked too many questions—such as the painting's reference. Led soon to
the catacombs of cooling systems, the art's viewed through small-scale
surveillance. A note on the Bacon reads: 'soon returned to a private
collection.' I ask, 'to whom?' She says it's confidential. An inconvenience:
they've left their Macs and papers. I am *seen*. They're whispering behind me,
making no eye contact. Given a stool in a room of sliding walls, three black
squares gaze at me. A triptych—side panels the same as the centrepiece.
A nuclear explosion in slow-mo, test paused. Chaos moves outwards,
inexorably. Behind me, I hear them laugh at the absurdity. This is my clown
painting, minus the clown. What remains is the felt background. A white
bezel hems in the dark matter. Is this the same as what goes on in asylums?
I'm immaterial in the scheme of things. All these happy deaths are making
me smile — under a time constraint like an exam. I want out: ready to end
this when you are. I have two minutes left—so what's the refrain? One
minute ... like a bomb disposal expert. My mind like a hand grenade.

∞

HAUNT

Then the sky fell in. I began to haunt him
with outmoded profile pics.
Then the dreams of dystopia started.
He couldn't get used to confinement
or he was too used to confinement.
He didn't yet know we need mirrors
to keep us sane.
Then it was Modernism 101
as he experimented with cutups.
Then he pasted me on his 5K screen
and copied me onto several drives.
Then jpegs appeared invasively
from his photo reel anniversaries.
Then he spliced one-minute clips
to upload a movie no-one could see.
I haunted him with my name on junk mail.
Then ectoplasm ran through my hands.
Then drugs and sex were outlets. *Tut.*
Then he loved other women. *Tut.*
Then they began to haunt him too.
Then the sink filled with botulism
and his beard grew. Then he began
to evaporate and mirrors all but disappeared.

MELANCHOLIA
After Albert György

Lake Geneva to my back
& my shadow cast, made digital.
This is how we know each other.
My arms bunched curtains
around a room you'll never enter.
Meanwhile, years happen.

A tree is a friend in winter:
its bareness & stark branches
reaching into organs.
My bare feet nailed to flags,
head downcast in the cleft
where light enters,
does nothing but enter.

Meanwhile, the bench on which
I sit stays zero centigrade.
My hand droops unheld
like most hands in this world.
Off in the distance
& through the window
of my torso are coloured bulbs,
dangling over the esplanade.

SVALBARD

I nearly went to Svalbard. That was before the news feature
on the shot polar bear, the result of an ice safari. I was off
to a conference on darkness. I didn't see the foxes on the
tundra, the aurora, or hear the paper on Verdi's operas. I
didn't buy a passport, told myself I didn't have the budget,
I couldn't afford it, 'there's no way you're going to enjoy it.'
I was disappointed to read the Radisson Blue was booked,
when I knew there was no hovercraft involved. I explored
Google Maps: whether or not the venue was in the Arctic
Circle. I imagined my legs like tripods scrunching through
snow. I imagined mittens fused to my flesh, thumbs stuck,
my 4G useless. I began to picture the trip like a film with a
soundtrack featuring a theremin, scenes like a comic strip.

It started with my visits to an anechoic chamber. I wanted
to hear my pulse in my brain, reach stars on my retina, get
as close to death as a sound lab allows. I was obsessed with
Orpheus. I was depressed: talk of Charon, placing an obol
on the tongue. I was drawn to thoughts of lyres, chthonic
trials. I wondered where in Norway I'd taxi. A plane crash
was my fantasy: not to arrive in body. I opted out, read up
on polar bears, the ethics of carrying a rifle, & who should
be shot—you or me. 'If it was me, I'd let myself be mauled,
struck in the temple.' If I stayed my pain could play out like
an aeolian harp: a martyr through the insistence of my heart.

HOW THE UNIVERSE WILL END
After J.M.W. Turner

With torsion.

As if staring through a kaleidoscope.

I'm drawn to avalanches, storms,

end-of-the-world catastrophes.

Babble is doing its best to coalesce into sign & symbol,

make sense.

Heat death. Big rip. Vacuum decay. I learn the terms.

I can't help but see a wreck where a serpent is.

This yellow disc, a magnesium sun,

blues a vortex.

A nebula cleaved open like a heart in a butcher's.

Vermilion goes on expanding—like the universe.

SHADE AND DARKNESS
After J.M.W. Turner

Before the rainbow arrives, I learn your grandparents survived
the Holocaust, they were put in a nuthouse for exposing the truth.
I learn the kernel of abuse may be traced to dreams of deluge.
Such madness we couldn't see through, opaque as your eyes,
this surface steeped in Goethe's frozen music. Before the rainbow
arrives, I follow murmurations. Over waves, shore-birds glide,
spiralling, threatening a tailspin. I wonder which camp they were in,
whether it was Auschwitz. In your eyes, I saw the first abuse.
I tried to trace the madness back, patch over the abyss, finding sense
in this, abstract and opaque. I tried to thaw your music, release
the birds from their circular trance.

SEASCAPE
Before J.M.W. Turner

The sea has no reply—& I'm devastated. The sea is easily equated with God. It ushers the waves towards me. I want to know why the sea is reticent. Even the sea won't accept my roses. Each year at Perranporth it's the same. I lay out the roses & the waves don't seem to care. I can't say which way the tide is turning. My fingers are dinted by thorns. No, even the sea won't accept my roses. It keeps giving them back, each wave returning the gift—like she often did. Was that generosity gone too far or a kind of self-hate? A dozen roses on the sand. A grief unresolved since God has refused to bear witness. *Are you not yet ashamed?* I am stood Canute-like. I am a dolt. How can I expect to shame the sea with my tears? The sea is making me wonder if the sky & stars are really the inside of my brain. In which case *she's out there,* I think. Why do we say the sea is blue when it's really grey? It recedes now—one immense field of consciousness. I ask the sea again to *give her back, please.* The plea of mortals in their millions. It's familiar to the sea. I believe the sea will make an exception. The only way to know for sure is to wade out & find a rip current, evade lifeguards between flags. The surfers are souls having a near death experience. They've risked jellyfish & sharks, joyous in wetsuits, halfway towards the empyrean. A friend says my only hope is immanence. I am privy to the knowledge of what's happened. Ashes in the mica. While she's in everything—from beach huts to kayaks to Alsatians on leads—while the sea is a sadist & says: *now it's time to leave.*

THE ARIADNE SERIES
Alongside Giorgio de Chirico

Quiescence stretches out as though the surface
were a moon. In my yard a Mediterranean light.

Airlessness is a dead giveaway here.
When the riddle insists, I refuse to listen.

A morbid dreamer hunched over a picnic table.
The lassitude of flies: my morning alarm.

All the wanderings of nomads offer no respite.
To degenerate minds the painting has a migraine.

I draw a chalk line around a murdered body.
Here the Argonauts are left behind.

I reminiscence over architectural bananas, tailors'
dummies, the underused maths room ...

Lugubrious cats descend of no fixed address.
Extreme foreshortening: I'm floating mid-air.

To the barbecue clings the ghost of halloumi.
The vacated square: like school after term ends.

THE MOON ON MY UTERUS

I hide behind a cloud. The sky is starless. My face is a sheeted mirror.
    I give her pains. She reaches for blister packs.
They have no such thing as nano probes to eat away the trouble.
    In seven years, the skeleton will replenish itself.
I wear these mother-of-pearl colours & opal for the surgeon's torch.
    I rest on her uterus. I am a moonset. I stab her
though she thinks it's her dream's assassin.
    Behold my seas & hemispheres. Behold my tendrils of venom.
The bloodstream feeds me like a mouth. My shape is agape & fearless.
    I am the medusa that sleeps inside you.

HEART-SHAPED BRUISE
After Nan Goldin

Blindness was a life of bruises, stubbed toes on table legs.
The one on your back: a bruise the shape of a butterfly.
Nursing your flesh, I'd find a heart or Horse-head Nebula.

Since then, I've been searching for signs of evidence
in the vaguest places: how solace reflects off bluish forms.

Still, I'm left stranded this side, tasked with redrawing the lines.
In this white cube, I find burst capillaries in a montage
of screen-prints, overhear on the mezzanine how she thinks
butterflies recall when they were caterpillars.

On the day you slipped in the shower, I was too quick
to photograph the bruise, the butterfly, focus on your
blindness when I was always the blindest.

I was so in the moment I missed the omen:
wings of a dark angel spreading from your spinal column.

SEPULCHRAL
After Bernard Pierre Wolff

Rain on benches in gardens of remembrance
reflect small portions of sky.

A chimney in the distance, belching out blackness
as if part of some regime.

Give me stars as casual gifts.
I fear a plateau: no hill to climb.

Place me on a precipice.
Cut me down for lamentation.

Who's the angel? Her arm draped over her brow
& now fallen on marble.

Trees quiver gran mal seizures.
No-one offers stark witness:

a weight of words too heavy to lift.
No-one wants hearts anymore

or knows anything of myth.
In a corner a columbarium calls.

Arches like ventricles I'll hide behind.
Kneeling on my catafalque

she'll let her tears escape their walls.

REFLEXION
After Christian Boltanski

[verso]

I am standing in front of four hundred black mirrors, nine wheeled racks
with suspended transparencies on cloth sheets.

I am lost in the twentieth century—which came to an end on 9/11.

That day in student halls I saw a movie on a plasma screen. Who will
brand this atrocity?

Earlier I heard of chopped limbs in Rwanda, of Kosovo bombs.

I learned what collateral damage means. History was full of warnings—
I didn't heed them.

[recto]

& now reflected: these shrouds, archives—or elsewhere dangling mobiles
made seemingly of metal & wire—puppet theatres throwing shades off
the highest shelf. Or sometimes cadavers, witches or dark automata, suspended
under interrogation lamps—for curators or the rich. All the anonymous faces
are filed in greyscale, mosaics on the walls of a gallery. I cannot find myself
in artefacts, nor accept the horror of this happening still, with the size reduced
down to your empty shoes, your hats in a trunk, your ring: everything a witness.

LOVERS
After Nancy Spero

This, I'm told, is the inverse
side of the androgyne, how lovers
lie apart with no skin contact.
How lovers are mere outlines,
or here they're solarised
as if scorched on a wall. How lovers
never belong to one another—
lovers don't know each other,
& sex is a way of growing apart.
I say that lovers rely on bodies,
they wrestle with futile lungs.
They spread on every surface.
Once lovers, now we are love,
& here it fills with a thousand suns.

HAIBUN

I'm a figurine. I sit in the park—like the trees, I seek thinness. Finally, I know where leaves go, having thought long by the pavilion. Dreams are abstract paintings: many visitations, no meaning. I see trees of limbs: in-patients. They reach beyond the stillness. I witness cribs, scooters, smiling chaps on fathers' shoulders. Leaves under shoes. And now under the downpour, I pass tennis courts—where thoughts go to nearly-girlfriends ... Instead, I spend time with doves. I'm in touch with such things. I clutch my cup: almond tea from a take-away kiosk. I see clouds, the shapes they make: each are *ciphers* if only we cover our ears. Sundays for the bereaved. A winter photo. I follow sticks, dog-leads. I sit again. Feel the curve of my pelvis on rain-sodden chairs. All is lamplit. Once more by the warden's hut. The dream is stalled. Where she's a wraith of past summers, lives in distant cities.

*

She haunts. Hangs up when I ring her number.
She's bruised by her passage from one world to another.

GHOST
After Rachel Whiteread

Like how voile serves as a lens,
through which bare sycamores
in late afternoon sun
bestow an image.

I recall in childhood the spectra
falling on enamel tubs,
the poignant one-off precision
of light on a wall.

I still find this sacred light is love,
where love lands
on your altar.
Look closer, you say
don't falter, here is love.

THRESHOLD

Through your two o'clock aperture
you'd see a flash of pink hyacinths.

I crouch by your angel on the sill
& squint: your vision a colour field.

No graven image on your retina
just a corner-of-the-eye apparition.

I listen & get so far. I close my eyes
then gaze through the rippled glass.

I strip away detail, figure, form, till
almost I reach you, *together we're torn.*

DEVOTION

I know the afterlife is to be dispensed
through sites on the Internet.

I collect her prints and jpegs
while found feathers on the pavement are kept.

I beat my heart with my palm so she can hear.
Despite the silence it's a standoff to the end.

∞

CONCERNING THE SPIRITUAL
After Wassily Kandinsky

are you in this image

        making it sing

while eyes are blind

        lush colour harmonies

clashing

        sunlit through blinds

a music box plays

        reds and yellows

gifting vision

        hemmed in by a frame

how your genius

        finds itself blind

like a lone beggar

        with open palms

seeing where lines go

        whether they join stars

while my love

        you were never blind

an artist living off

        her instincts

your quantum mind

        giving the impression

of seeing while blind

        seeing through one eye

your world like this canvas

        your message

going haywire

        in patches and shards

hardly blind

                            just mute to the outside

Kim you were loveable

                            due to your limits

your work unfinished

                            you'd say open your eyes

just write

                            throw open your blinds

Holding on to our last-gasp hours—whispered *I love yous*
in my ear. Once more, you inch up to my lobe, earring hole,
up close doing your best to compress our future in a phrase,
a tense, something to last under lids. That will pass through
your dawns, your evenings. *I love yous* as I squeeze myself
through a needle head. To blackness or birth-light. Our pact
in place. The last things: a rosary, a sponge on my tongue,

a pan flute, a hypodermic. Frankincense plumes in a room
we can't mention. My waxen suit lifts to a halo. My eyebrow
twitches *yes, we are still fusion*—hands entwined, fasting.
As we were: a ritual of ribbons. I mouth the too-late advice:
evacuate. You said we had lightning in a jar. The tragedy is
you meant it. Now sparks arc like sea-drenched arms. How
is it possible to have the final say? *I love yous* back and forth

while the mind slides doors; ancestors arrive. We've tried
to wear out the will—puncture it through. Find a way out
with a maze-trail. My promise of a comeback or getaway
hurts your faith: the cliche of how *energy never dies*. The sun
does through its discharge. Shrinks to a cinder while you wait.
For now you are Earth bound, stuck to lobules and ducts—
while I notice the neon, pulled up and up. Away and tied

to a kite you can't remember. *I love yous*—to fade. Your kiss
on my fringe. If only I could pin this cord with a paper clip.
Minutes before my lips stitch, the sloughing of skin. Unzip.
Escape valve firing. Perhaps a zygote the start to seal it. For cells
to divide as they should. Stop once done. Perhaps when clouds
slow down, things will seem real. Listen: my disappearance
makes so much sense. Don't worry—it's not even an issue.

ANNIVERSARY

The season assails me: flashbacks—daffodils linked
with nausea, pinks of cherry blossom fallen
in my stomach's pit, the sickness of spring evocations ...

Like surgical gauze left behind, hurt comes in waves—
the burn of how we abandon each other.
When our film clips are stitched everything is vaudeville.

Skinless I drift through the manicured beds
through bluebells by the haunted parsonage.
I ask, 'God, what do all the symbols mean?'—

robins that land on benches, distant ice-cream vans'
nostalgia. Everything a beautiful catastrophe.
The rays of May penetrate. Spring blossoms,

torn crate paper ready for decoupage. As if the body's
stasis chamber knows the date—
anniversaries through springtime, through springtime ...

Are we on pause or between sentences?
'Acceptance' is a word like the cigarette scar on my arm—
the scar my watch face hides.

The mind says it's create or die—create or die.
I cling to our love like a rodeo. I write your lines
sous rature. And still, we are star-crossed:

you on your side, me on mine.

WINTER GHAZAL

Over bed covers of snow, I go in search of your eyes.
As the sun funnels through the glaze, in dreams I never
find your eyes. A new day without you. So, I caress your
pillow's furrow, a rivulet that carries my scent to your
half-moon eyes. I inspect marks on my flesh, hashtags
of ruffled sheets, temporary tattoos I can't bear to lose.
In the mind's eye, I bag your fingernail & wipe lipstick
off the mirror. As the sun fingers your fabrics, I learn
to revive your eyes. On waking this morning, I hear a
music box melody. Like you're a phantom limb, I feel
you still, your eyes, our clinch, our skin-to-skin. I cling
to your sarong, slung over a hook, untouched. How I
was braille under your eyes. & Kim, the wicker screen
is filtering light, it falls on the sill, on your gift of the
angel harp—& how you'd smile at this.

VANISHING POINT
After Hiroshi Sugimoto

I'm staring across a lake of tar—perhaps on Titan
where the lakes are made of diesel, where the lakes
are a dark carpet once seen from a foetal position.

This line I liken to a veil. It separates our lives—
unlike the veil you wore churchless on Primrose Hill.
We shared an organza canopy draped over love-smiles.

Sleep is a flurry of shadows. I keep voicemails
about lost keys, while the sirens unsettle you.

This is how our relationship endures: you exist
behind a firewall
                    where a montage of our movie
        is playing somewhere over the curve of a satellite.
            It seems to be saying that the dead are here,
                watching us,
                            but they cannot interfere.

ETERNAL MOVEMENT
After Idris Khan

Everything depends on the problem of consciousness.

If the body is like a car, who is the driver?

I cannot believe in the random firing of synapses.

If all your neurones were more than stars in the galaxy
our hearts, I imagine, are quantum entangled.

If I collapse the wave function, when you appear
through sleep, you're *real*.

If the universe is infinite, I just need to learn to travel far enough.

I need to know between us is one instant.

It gives me hope: you appear as a ghost.

Our dreams are the equivalent of dark matter.

Could it be death is a place we become increasingly self-aware?

Could it be in the empty space between atoms
everything about you is recorded in some etheric plane?

If from the perspective of a photon the Big Bang is happening still
I believe it's possible: we will meet again.

END OR BEGINNING
After Idris Kahn

I know you have trouble   with afterlives
since all your dead   never cared for you
though when the silkscreens are   like this
firing stars   from one immense nucleus
one super dense heartbeat   please believe

the brain does more than scan itself   as a
survival technique   that in the end not all
proof needs a witness   the pineal gland
tethering us to a place   both near and far

others refer to a room   of velvet sheets
where clocks implode   love wraps around
us like a cloak   *All is well* booms the voice
and a pinhole appears   in the ceiling
drawing us closer   to the distant song

'Beginning or End' paraphrases Jacques Derrida's idea that our death is the one thing we can truly own. This proposal is conveyed in *Donner la mort* (translated as *The Gift of Death*).

The word 'Metanoia' refers to a transformative change of heart or spiritual conversion.

The word 'qualia' in 'Vir Heroicus Sublimis' indicates a quality or property as perceived or experienced by a person.

'Shroud' includes a line that offers a new spin on Ludwig Wittgenstein's belief that death is not a human experience.

'Black Square Redux' is a response to the ideas of Nikolai Fyodorov and transhumanism.

'Cold Room' refers to Ecclesiastes 1:9: 'What has been will be again, what has been done will be done again; there is nothing new under the sun.'

'True Belief Belongs to the Realm of Real Knowledge' is based on the work of David Bohm, who contributed unorthodox ideas to quantum theory. It also refers to Marcus Aurelius in comparing time to a river.

'Severance' is inspired by Emmanuel Swedenborg's *Heaven and its Wonders and Hell from Things Heard and Seen* (1758).

The phrase 'science is a candle in the dark' in 'Tenebrae' is taken from the subtitle of Carl Sagan's book *The Demon-Haunted World*.

The word 'plenum' in 'Robert Rauschenberg's *Untitled*' refers to a space filled with matter.

The phrase 'Night Sea Journey' is inspired by Carl Jung and relates to the idea of Nekyia: a rite by which ghosts are summoned and questioned about the future.

'Abstraction' refers to Gerard Manley Hopkins' idea of inscape (defined as 'the unique inner nature of a person or object as shown by a work of art, especially a poem'). This poem also mentions Gilbert Ryle's phrase 'ghost in the machine', which he used in his description of René Descartes' mind-body dualism.

The word 'Vantablack' in 'Black Square' is a brand name for a class of super-black coatings with total hemispherical reflectances below 1.5% in the visible spectrum.

'Nocturne' references a lawsuit between J.A.M. Whistler and the art critic John Ruskin.

'Sunrise with Sea-monsters' hints at the apocryphal final words of J.M.W. Turner: 'The sun is God'.

'Lessons on How to View a Mondrian' began as a found poem and re-presents a *HuffPost* article by the art critic James Elkins: 'How to Look at Mondrian' (2010).

'Memento Mori' contains a reference to anamorphosis: an optical illusion where an image appears to be distorted when seen from the usual vantage point but appears normal when viewed from a specific angle.

'The Misophonic Brain' refers to misophonia: a condition in which individuals experience intense anger and disgust when confronted with sounds made by other human beings.

'My Series of Long Goodbyes' includes the word 'retinitis'. This is my shortening of *retinitis pigmentosa* (a group of rare eye diseases that affect the retina).

'Private Viewing' was written *in situ* in the Whitworth Art Gallery's holdings, Manchester.

'Svalbard' refers to an anechoic chamber: a piece of equipment that screens out almost all light and sound.

'How the Universe Will End' is inspired by Gilles Deleuze writing on J.M.W. Turner's final paintings in *The Anti-Oedipus: Capitalism and Schizophrenia.*

'Sepulchral' is also an homage to the music of Joy Division and New Order.

'Anniversary' is a horticultural ekphrasis in response to Parsonage Gardens, Didsbury.

The opening line in 'Eternal Movement' is influenced by the work of David Chalmers and the hard problem of consciousness.

ACKNOWLEDGEMENTS

Many thanks to the editors of the following magazines and journals where some of the poetry in this book first appeared: *Abridged, After..., Agenda, Apricot Press, Bending Genres, Black Bough Poetry, Damnation, Dark Winter Literary Magazine, Dreich, Empyrean Literary Magazine, Feral, Fevers of the Mind, Impossible Archetype, Indigo Literary Journal, Ink, Sweat and Tears, Leon Literary Review, Lighthouse, Meniscus, Metachrosis Literary Magazine, Morning Fruit, On the High, Pidgeonholes, Pinhole Poetry, Poetry Ireland Review, Red Tree Review, Rough Diamond, Southword, Surging Tide, Sweet Lit, The Alchemy Spoon, The Ekphrastic Review, The High Window, The Light Ekphrastic, The North, The Shore, The Storms, The Waxed Lemon, West Trade Review*, and *Worcester Review*.

'The Ariadne Series' appears in *Little Thorns in the Back of Your Throat Are the Hardest to Remove*, an anthology edited by Rebecca Rijsdijk, *Sunday Mornings at the River*, October 2022.

'Dark Clouds Storm Blue' was reprinted in the *Fevers of the Mind Poetry, Art & Music*, Issue 10 anthology, edited by David L. O'Nan and HilLesha O'Nan, Spring 2024.

'Ghost' appears in the *Black Bough Poetry: Christmas and Winter Anthology*, edited by Matthew M. Smith, Issue 4, Winter 2023.

The introductory epigraph is taken from *The Brothers Karamazov* by Fyodor Dostoyevsky.

I'd also like to thank the following people for their support and encouragement: Aaron Kent and *Broken Sleep Books*, Cate Myddleton-Evans, Dónall Maccathmhaoill, Helen Mort, Helen Ivory, Helen Tookey, Tamar Yoseloff, Patricia McCarthy, Jane Yeh, and Siobhan Campbell.

Thank you to Kim, Christine, Nick, and others who have passed on, who have nevertheless felt present and provided me with inspiration.

Thank you to my beloved, Rowan.

LAY OUT YOUR UNREST